MW01601805

It's Okay to be
SQUARE...

and other wise platitudes

*"The stories we tell ourselves
become the life that we live."*

JUDY KAY MAUSOLF

WAYNE KERR, DDS, MAGD

OTHER BOOKS BY THE AUTHOR

Ten Tips to the Top!
A primer for the successful dental practice.

When Life Needs a Sticky Note...
words of inspiration during challenging times

BIG Success for Small Business
...a primer for the entrepreneur

When Mom and Dad Need Help...
caring for parents and loved ones

Wise Words
...from Lessons Learned

TABLE *of* CONTENTS

PREFACE

I don't know what was going through your mind during the earliest days of the pandemic, but I struggled greatly to grasp the enormity of what was happening. Within the span of just a few weeks, every professional commitment I'd made for 2020, vanished into thin air! It was late March when, sitting at my desk and staring at a blank computer screen, I realized I needed to change my mindset.

I pulled out a stack of post-it notes and began writing words of thanks and positive thoughts, placing them all over the walls of my study. "I'm thankful for the roof over my head and for a safe place to sleep each night." "I'm thankful for my family and for our health." "I'm thankful that I can put food on the table." "I know we'll all get through this and that the future is still bright."

This exercise so elevated my spirits, I decided to share some of my thoughts with others and wrote *"When Life Needs a Sticky Note... words of inspiration during challenging times."* This compilation of essays was so well received by friends, family, colleagues, and others, I elected to author a second book, *"Wise Words... from Lessons Learned."* Once again, I was pleasantly surprised by its popularity.

"It's Okay to be **SQUARE**" offers additional insight into living well, even when we're challenged daily as never before. It illustrates that it's most important to accept yourself for who you are, fill your mind with positive thoughts, find joy every day, and acknowledge that you can't save the world, though you might try.

I hope you find my thoughts and essays meaningful, instructional, and most importantly, inspirational. Enjoy!

All the best to you and yours,

— *Wayne Kerr, DDS, MAGD*

CHAPTER 1

Don't Try to be Something You're Not

"Son, it's okay to be square."

J. C. KERR, JR.

DON'T TRY TO BE
SOMETHING YOU'RE NOT

Two years ago (long before the pandemic), I attended my fiftieth high school class reunion in the small, central Florida town in which I was raised. The well-planned weekend events were an absolute blast, and I experienced great joy as I was reunited with old friends.

The opening weekend event was an outdoor patio reception that took place in the late Friday afternoon sunshine. The air was warm, the pinot grigio was cold, and the mood was festive. Past friendships were renewed, old stories were retold, and hugs and kisses were freely exchanged! At some point, I just paused, leaned against a brick wall, and took it all in, thinking just how fortunate I was to enjoy this exceptional moment in life.

Late in the day, we lined up for a buffet dinner of pulled-pork bar-b-que with all the trimmings. About that time, a couple of my former classmates got in line behind me and exclaimed, "Why,

Wayne Kerr! How great to see you! You always were the *life of the party!*" Although I grinned back at them, I thought to myself, "That's really funny, because I was *never invited* to a party!" And that's true!

I remember working in the yard with my dad one Saturday morning while in junior high and complaining to him that I wasn't part of the "in crowd." Dad asked me why that was important to me, and all I could think to say at the time was, "Well, *they're cool.*" And then he asked me if being "cool" would improve my grades or help me get into the college of my choice. Hmmmm...

Knowing that his response disappointed me, he put down his shovel, placed his hand on my shoulder, looked me right in the eyes and said, "Son, it's okay to be square." "Square" of course, was the Sixties synonym for "nerd." I gotta say Dad's comment hit me kind of hard at the time, but his message was meaningful. You see, I was a pimple-faced kid dressed by Sears who held up his britches with a one-size, fits-all stretch belt. And I loved school, especially the sciences. Why in the world would I be considered *cool* or be part of the "in crowd...?"

The life lesson I learned from my father that day is that it's important to be true to yourself. It's always fine to seek self-improvement, but trying to be something you're not, may lead to disappointment, loss of self-esteem, depression or failure.

The reunion weekend included a Saturday morning prayer breakfast honoring those classmates who were no longer with us. As the video presentation rolled on and tears silently streaked down my cheeks, it never occurred to me whether my lost classmates were "cool" or not. It only mattered that those friendships were gone forever and that I would never again enjoy their company.

If it's your dream to climb Mount Everest, go for it! If you hope one day to be Miss America, good luck! If you still want to earn that Master's degree, hit the books! But if you're just "you," and you're happy with who you are and where you are in life, celebrate that! Be true to yourself and to others, but don't worry about being someone that someone else thinks you should be! You're you, that's enough, and that's *great!* All the best!

CHAPTER 2

Be Slow to Anger

"Family is not an important thing.
It's everything."

MICHAEL J. FOX

BE SLOW TO ANGER

We grew up poor, but as kids, we didn't know that. We always had a roof over our heads and a safe place to sleep each night. We had loving parents and food on the table. And we always had each other. Looking back on those "Wonder Years" of the Fifties and Sixties, I now realize that we were rich as hell. Yeah, we had pretty much everything that mattered then…. and matters now.

My brother, two and a half years older than me, was my best friend growing up. We shared everything: candy, secrets, adventures, and – yes – our toys. We only had three our entire childhood, but they were the best toys available and the only ones we needed: Erector Set, Tinker Toy, and Lincoln Logs. And there wasn't anything that we couldn't do or build with our youthful imaginations and those magnificent toys! Wahoo!

We became masters at creating structures that combined the elements of all three toys and proudly presented them to our parents for approval and praise.

I was convinced that my brother and I would ultimately become engineers and design innovations that would change the world. (A boy can dream, right…?)

One Saturday morning, my brother built the most elaborate structure I'd ever seen using only Lincoln Logs. It was an architectural wonder — complete with a cantilevered deck — and I was most impressed. I was also jealous and wanted to "outdo" him. Dad, however, was out of town working on a company project, and so the structure stood for days, then weeks, waiting for his return.

I don't remember why, but my brother and I got into a fight over something, and I allowed my anger to get the best of me. In the blink of an eye and with a mighty swing of my right hand, I destroyed his beautiful Lincoln Log creation. Dad would never see it, and my brother cried.

I never played with our set of Lincoln Logs after that. I was too ashamed. But the incident eventually brought us closer together because we ultimately realized that brotherhood is far more durable and meaningful than a stack of Lincoln Logs. It means loving, honoring, and respecting each other — and each other's achievements — throughout a lifetime.

CHAPTER 3

Find Joy Everyday

"Get busy living... or get busy dying."

RED (MORGAN FREEMAN) FROM
SHAWSHANK REDEMPTION

FIND JOY EVERYDAY

I turned twenty the day Georgia Tech played Tulane on Grant Field. The torrential rain turned the grass field into a quagmire and, as a cheerleader on the sideline for Tech, I became covered in mud. It was a great day, an exciting Tech victory, and an exhilarating experience which filled my youthful heart with unabashed joy!

I'm thankful for that memory and of numerous other life experiences which have brought me great joy. My son-in-law refers to such occasions as *"goosebump memories."* How appropriate.

But it seems to me that there aren't enough days in our lives like my twentieth birthday, and I sometimes wonder why...? My theory is that we are so busy "doing" that we often fail to "live," and miss many of life's simple pleasures which could add joy to each day. And that's a shame.

I was certainly guilty of this as a young practitioner. For the first eight years of my career, I served so many community and professional entities, I was out twenty nights per month after long days at the office serving a variety of organizations. It's important to point out that many of those activities brought me personal satisfaction and a sense of accomplishment, but my schedule was exhausting and robbed me of "goosebump" opportunities and time with my family.

There's an old saying that "Yesterday is history, tomorrow just a mystery, but today is a gift, which is why it's called the *present.*" So, find ways to enjoy each day, for tomorrow is never promised. Take in its beauty, enjoy the little things, celebrate small victories, love what you do, find reasons to laugh, and reflect upon your many blessings. Each day can become one of "goosebump memories" if we focus on *living* rather than *doing.*

CHAPTER 4

Stop Talkin' Trash

"A positive mindset leads to a positive life!"

WAYNE KERR, DDS, MAGD

STOP TALKIN' TRASH

It was an unseasonably hot Saturday afternoon for March in Atlanta. The ballroom was packed, the overflow crowd of attendees lined the walls, and the hotel's air-conditioning system was woefully inadequate. The great motivational speaker Zig Ziglar leapt from one side of the dais to the other as he entertained, enthralled, and engaged us with his presentation.

As beads of sweat trickled down his forehead, Ziglar paused mid-sentence and made a great show of mopping his face with the handkerchief he pulled from his back pocket. He removed his suit coat, carefully folded it, placed it upon the table before him, and then asked, "Hot, ain't it?" As we chuckled in agreement, he lifted a pitcher of ice water off the table, held it high above a water glass, and slowly poured the icy stream until the glass was nearly full. After returning the pitcher to the table, he drank the entire glass of water, set it down, expressed great satisfaction with a loud, "Ahhhhhh," and wiped his mouth with the back of his hand. Wordlessly he scanned his audience from one side of the room to the other and then asked, *"Thirsty, aren't ya'?"* It's my guess that, at that moment, most of us in the room would have gladly given Zig ten bucks for what was left in that pitcher of water and felt that we'd gotten a pretty good deal.

A true master-of-communication, Ziglar reminded us that day that much of who we are or become in life is influenced by who we spend time with and that which we put into our mind. Most of us are more than capable of avoiding toxic people that suck the life right out of us, but few among us consistently feed our brain the positive messages and affirmations it needs to build confidence and enhance our self-esteem.

The problem is that our brain believes what we tell it, and what we tell ourselves is often negative. I call it "trash talk," and it's difficult to control, for it's human nature to be self-critical when we do something that disappoints us. I know I'm guilty. The other morning, I forgot that I put my coffee cup in the microwave to reheat the portion that was left and then knocked it over spilling its contents everywhere when I attempted to place a second item in it for heating. And what did I immediately say to myself....? "You are *so* stupid!" And my brain said, "Yes, you are stupid...." Trash talk...

A favorite tale recounted by Ziglar further illustrates the point. He describes a late arrival to a crowded conference who pauses on the way into the meeting room to pour a cup of coffee and load a couple of danish pastries onto a plate. As he balances breakfast in one hand and grips his briefcase in the other, he tells himself

"I'm going to spill this" while navigating his way across the room to an open chair. Sure enough, he catches a foot on the leg of a chair and spills his coffee and danish onto the floor. And then he says to himself, "I *knew* I was going to spill this." And Ziglar observes, "Of course he was going to spill it because he told himself that he was."

Norman Vincent Peale is perhaps the sage most famously associated with the power of positive thinking, but it's Zig Ziglar who reminds us to "get a check-up from the neck-up" to "eliminate our stinkin' thinkin'." Again, that's easier said than done.

My suggestion is to begin each day with gratitude and fill your mind with positive thoughts (affirmations). "I'm smart." "I like myself." "I'm really good at what I do." "Today is going to be a great day." And, if you find negative thoughts creeping into your mind, just turn them off and say, "I'm better than that!"

The bottom line here is that we should be kind to ourselves. We're not perfect and we'll continue to fall short of our personal expectations from time to time, but we shouldn't beat ourselves up over such failures. As Paulo Coelho once observed, "You are what you believe yourself to be!"

Stop talkin' trash and get on with your life!

CHAPTER 5

Embrace Opportunity

*"All our dreams can come true if we have
the courage to pursue them."*

WALT DISNEY

EMBRACE OPPORTUNITY

Being thrifty, I rarely spend a great deal of money on a pair of shoes. But, some years ago, I purchased a beautiful pair of ColeHaan dress shoes at an outlet store. They became my favorite pair to wear with a coat and tie, and I wore them out time and again. In fact, I had them resoled three times!

I remember that the last time I took them to be repaired at our local shoe repair shop, the cobbler told me that he was closing his store at the end of the year and that I'd need to prepay for the repair in cash. Although I was happy to do so, I asked him why he was closing his very successful repair shop. His answer stunned me when he said, "I want to retire and have no buyer for my business."

Okay, so I don't possess the world's greatest business mind, but I wondered why the repairman's right-hand man wasn't buying the business and I asked him. He said that his boss wanted $500 to buy the business, but he couldn't take the risk.

Are you kidding me? I borrowed $40,000 to open my first practice in 1978, and the price tag to open a new practice today exceeds six figures!! $500, really? The cobbler's assistant had the skills and experience necessary to be successful and was being offered his own business for virtually nothing. He was, in fact, only paying for a lathe, an awl, a few hand tools, and some remaining inventory.

When I asked him why he "couldn't take the risk," he said, "I'm used to getting a paycheck and don't know what I'd do without one." Wow.

The years have passed, the old shop is still closed, and the building which once housed a thriving local business is falling into disrepair. In my humble opinion, purchasing his employer's business was a life-changing opportunity for the young man, but one that he "lost" by not taking advantage of it. What a shame for him and for our community, as we are still without a local shoe repair shop.

If you wish to own a small business one day, listen to your heart. Write your Vision Plan. Believe in yourself. And take those steps necessary to make all your dreams come true... As the old saying goes, *opportunity knocks but once!*

CHAPTER 6

Don't Burn Bridges

"Successful businesses are built upon product excellence, customer service, and personal relationships. Deliver excellence in product and service, but nourish and maintain those key relationships, based upon trust and mutual respect."

WAYNE KERR, DDS, MAGD

DON'T BURN BRIDGES

I remember, as a teen, helping a friend (who was part of the "in crowd") achieve his goal, and afterward being treated as though we were complete strangers. I didn't understand and whined about it to my dad. "I thought we were friends," I exclaimed! "Well, we're not friends anymore!" But Dad wisely advised, "Son, don't burn any bridges you don't have to burn." Yeah...

There's a lot of truth to that, because we never know where the road of life will lead us... Decades later, during my career, I had a personal disagreement with a professional friend but realized that he was a valued member of my network, and therefore, I didn't "burn that bridge." Indeed, my teammates and I continued to refer our patients to his practice for specialty care. And that was the right thing to do, not so much for me, but for the patients that we served.

But sometimes events and circumstances cause bridges to burn by themselves! Just a few years before I retired, the monitor in my consultation room died and needed replacement. I found exactly what I wanted at Target for $300. But, before buying it, I called my tech support company and asked what they'd charge to replace it. When I learned that they could do it for only fifty dollars more, I elected to have them take care of it, as I always liked supporting those businesses which supported me.

Imagine my surprise when a television (in a previously opened carton) was installed *instead* of a monitor and imagine my displeasure when the graphics were illegible! When I called to complain, I was told that I needed new cabling. *What? The old cabling worked!* So, new cabling was installed at a cost of $600 to make my new "monitor" work!

As you might suspect, I was less than pleased! I could have solved the problem myself for $300, but instead paid nearly $1,000 to my local tech firm to resolve the issue. They made a very simple situation unnecessarily difficult and expensive for me by installing the wrong product and then pretending that it was my problem to fix, not theirs. Yeah, that ended our relationship. And when I fired them, I was "less than nice." That bridge burned and it was gone forever.

Whether in our personal or professional lives, it's necessary to remember that relationships are important, and not to be meaninglessly squandered on a whim. Relationships are built over time and never should be abandoned due to a fit of anger or misunderstanding. Having said that, however, sometimes a relationship implodes through no fault of your own, and it's necessary to walk away.

If you're thinking about "burning a bridge," evaluate the situation carefully. The relationship you are about to end might be one you wished you had saved for the future. But if that bridge is already on fire, it's not your responsibility to launch a bucket brigade to save it.

CHAPTER 7

Build Value

"Values give rise to attitudes... your values
are not merely those things you talk about in
church or refer to when someone asks you
what you believe in. Your values are deeply
held beliefs about what is important,
precious, or sacred to you."

EMMETT MILLER

BUILD VALUE

My family has long had a love affair with HoneyBaked hams. Thanksgiving, Christmas, Easter... pretty much any holiday or large family gathering provided the excuse necessary to purchase the wonderful delicacy.

Recently I dropped by the store to pick up two bottles of their delightful Hickory Honey Mustard. Even without the ham, it makes just about any sandwich taste better. Armed with a ten-dollar bill, I was surprised when the clerk told me my total was $12.84. I said, "Wow! That's expensive mustard," to which she replied, "Yes, it is."

I kept waiting to hear the next sentence. You know, the one where she says, *"But it's worth it!"* But she didn't say that. She basically just told me that her mustard was overpriced.

As a young practitioner, I was quite "price sensitive," but set extremely high standards for patient care. It was critically important to me that each patient served received a "mountaintop" experience from start to finish, and that only the finest materials and devices would be used in delivering their care. And my fees reflected that.

Early in my career, however, I employed a young lady who failed to understand that. Although she worked in my business office, she was terrible at collecting payment for services rendered. Because it was necessary for her to succeed at this important task, I pulled out a couple of training manuals from my office library and shared with her the proper techniques and appropriate verbal skills to improve her technique.

When there was no significant improvement in collections the following month, I challenged her regarding her continued failure to collect payment at the time of service. She just looked at me and said, "I can't ask them to pay their bill. You're not worth it." That was her last day.

It never occurred to me that one of my own employees – who happily accepted a better than average salary with numerous benefits – thought my fees were too high. As I reflect upon that experience, I realize it was my failure to properly lead my team and communicate the practice's core values that contributed to it.

You see, those core values were clearly spelled out in my office policy manual, but – to my employees – they were just words. Without sharing our common values through open communication and building a vision that we all "owned," they would remain "just words."

That lesson in leadership was a hard one for me, but one of great value. In time, my practice attracted quality employees who shared with me a common vision for providing patients with a "mountaintop" experience from beginning to end. We maintained high ethical standards, built long-lasting, personal relationships, established trust, and took whatever time was necessary to properly educate those we served before initiating any recommended treatment. In short, we built value for the services we rendered.

Not only were we paid for those services, but we were rewarded by patients who made and kept future preventive care appointments and built our practice by referring to us their families and friends. Clearly, building value for one's products and/or services is critically important to the success of any business. I wonder if the lovely young clerk at HoneyBaked Ham has figured that out yet...

CHAPTER 8

Don't Say It...

"Discretion is the better part of valor."

FALSTAFF, KING HENRY THE FOURTH,
WILLIAM SHAKESPEARE

("Caution is preferable to rash bravery.")

DON'T SAY IT...

One of the best pieces of advice passed on to me by my paternal grandmother was "If you can't say something nice about someone, it's best not to say anything at all." Remembering that at a critical moment in my youth probably saved me a lot of trouble...

In hindsight, the situation was really kind of funny, because I'm not much of a golfer. In fact, my idea of golf at the time was a double date with a buddy at a miniature golf course on Highway 17-92. But it was my senior year at Winter Park High, and a classmate had six tickets to the Orlando Open.

So, six of us piled into his '64 Mustang (pre-seatbelt) and spent a gorgeous spring afternoon watching Arnold Palmer, Jack Nicklaus, Tom Weiskopf and other greats play the game. I've got to admit, we all had a blast. There was only one problem. We cut sixth period Physics to go.

Through twelve years of public school, I missed one day (wisdom tooth surgery) and cut one class. Yep. It was *that* class! Two weeks before graduation no less.

As we took our seats in Physics the next day, our instructor, a former Air Force colonel, called out our names. He told us each to pull out a sheet of paper, write our name on it, and turn it in. Once we had complied, he advised us that each of us had failed the "pop test," and would lose one letter grade. And we did.

Then he asked us what we had learned from cutting his class. When none of us answered, he called my name. "Kerr, what did you learn from this experience?" And *that's* when my grandmother's loving advice kicked in. What I wanted to say was "You have a fragile ego, you're vindictive, and you abuse your authority." What I said was, "I guess I shouldn't have cut your class" (which was precisely the right answer and the one he wanted to hear).

Ironically, I earned two "D's" and a "B" in three quarters of Physics as a college freshman. Maybe I should have skipped more than one class in high school since I apparently didn't learn too much about the subject while I was there...

CHAPTER 9

Invest in Yourself

"The quality of a person's life is in direct proportion to their commitment to excellence, regardless of their chosen field of endeavor."

VINCE LOMBARDI

INVEST IN YOURSELF

I'll be the first to admit that it was far easier bagging groceries in strong paper bags that held their shape than it is to do so using today's pleomorphic plastic. I know, because I was a bagboy in the Sixties and took great pride in what I did. The brief training I received from my manager, Jim Butler, was simple but effective: double bag for heavy items, cans on the bottom with light items like crackers or cookies on top, pack cold things together, raw meat separately, and bread and eggs get special attention. So why is it that no one working in my grocery store knows that?

And when did cashiers forget how to make change? Not long ago, my grocery bill was $16.25. I gave the young lady $21.25 expecting a $5 bill in change. She handed the $1.25 back to me saying *"I only need the twenty."* When she counted out my $3.75 in change, I gave it back to her with the $1.25 that was still in my hand and asked her for a five. She just stared at me...

When the attitude of the employee clearly illustrates that he or she simply doesn't care to be better at what they do, I find fault with them. But when it's clear they've never been properly trained to perform at a higher level, I blame the employer. (Ask me how I know....).

As a completely inexperienced small-business owner in the late seventies, I made virtually every practice management mistake that can be made, including failing to properly train my young team. Since I only hired people with "experience," I (wrongly) assumed they'd intuitively know what to do! *Yeah, that worked well!*

In time, we all received the training needed to deliver patient services with high standards of excellence. Doing so, however, required commitment, focus, a shared future vision, and a significant financial investment. But it was clear to me that, if I was only going to be as good as my team, my team was going to be the very best.

That was an important lesson for me as a new employer, but one that served me well throughout my long career. It's important to always offer ones' clients or customers the very best products, services, and experiences possible. And that takes training as well as pride in what one does.

CHAPTER 10

Value Your Time

"If you don't value your time, no one else will."

J. C. KERR, JR.

VALUE YOUR TIME

A friend of mine recently recounted how being sequestered and working from home has helped her. It seems that she manages a large commercial property and, that by being off campus due to the pandemic, most of the "drop by and whine sessions" from various tenants have disappeared. Amazing! Is there something to be said about being "too available...?"

Allow me to recount a "less than wonderful" memory... It was my third year in practice, and I received notice of the death of a dear friend. I blocked out my schedule and arranged to leave my office in time to attend his funeral.

I finished my morning schedule on time, had a quick bite to eat, changed into a coat and tie, and left the office. As I approached my car, however, I was asked by a stranger if I was the doctor. When I affirmed that I was, he exclaimed that he had just broken a tooth, that he was in pain, and that he needed immediate help.

When I explained that I wasn't available and was headed to a funeral, he screamed "What kind of doctor are you? I'm in pain and you're ignoring me?"

Yeah, well, you know what happened.... I missed my dear friend's funeral because I stupidly agreed to see and care for someone I had never met, didn't know, and wasn't a patient of record. I provided phenomenal care, and, after assuring that there was no pulpal exposure and that the "patient" wasn't really in any pain, built a first-class, pin-retained amalgam crown-core build up. After that, he skipped out of the office without paying for the services I had rendered, and his phone number and address turned out to be false. I never saw him again.

That was another hard lesson for me. I had failed to honor the memory of a dear friend while providing professional services for someone who would never be a friend. That person, in fact, had stolen far more from me than my time, clinical expertise, or money... he had stolen my opportunity to say goodbye to someone I loved and respected.

Sometimes it's best not to be "too available," since you might miss something in your life that really matters. You know, like honoring a dear friend for a life filled with compassion and service to others.

EPILOGUE

You Can't
Save the World

"It's better to give than to receive."

JESUS, ACTS 20:35, THE BIBLE

EPILOGUE:

YOU CAN'T SAVE THE WORLD

I was sixteen years old when Mom and Dad bought ten acres of good old Florida scrubland just west of Orlando. The Little Econ River ran across the back quadrant and the acreage was covered with palmetto and scrub oak. Dad hired a local man looking for work (and me for the summer) to clear the palmetto and put up a barbed wire fence for the cattle he planned to raise.

The newly hired hand seemed to be a fine man but had no transportation and relied on others to get him to his odd jobs. Dad decided to resolve the problem by cosigning a loan for a used pickup truck and arranging for several other men from church to commit to hiring him for various jobs on a regular basis. As you might imagine, having his own truck and the promise of steady work, gave him a sense of pride and independence. And, for a while, everything worked like a charm.

The summer was hot and humid, and he and I sweated buckets grubbing out palmetto roots, digging fence post holes, and stringing barbed wire. Long before Gatorade and other sport drinks were available, we swallowed salt tablets and gallons of water to compensate for the fluids and minerals we lost. After weeks of strenuous work, the fence was completed, and Dad's "hired hand" moved on to another job. And that's when the trouble began.

It seems that a chain saw was needed to meet the needs of his next employer and the man asked my father if he could borrow his. Dad reluctantly agreed and told him he needed it back in two weeks. But two weeks came and went, and the saw wasn't returned. When Dad confronted the laborer and asked for the saw, he was told that it had broken, and was in the shop for repair.

So, Dad went to Snodgrass Hardware, the only repair shop in town, to inquire about his saw only to discover that it wasn't there. In fact, Dad found his saw, in perfect working condition, at the local pawn shop. It had apparently been sold for some extra cash, and the man's dishonesty caused him to lose many of the odd jobs that had been lined up for him as well as the opportunity to earn an income.

Some months later, the bank called my father to make good on the note he cosigned because it was past due. Dad paid off the loan to avoid damage to his credit rating but terminated his relationship with the man he had tried to help.

Guess I didn't learn much from my father's experience because, as a young small business owner, I very nearly made the same mistake. I hired a local woman in need of work to clean my office each week, but she relied on others for a ride. So, after a three-month trial to assess her skills and dependability, I bought her a used car and provided her with steady work for more than two years. The arrangement worked well until she hocked her car for a "pay day loan" to post bail for her daughter's release from jail. Although she pleaded with me to "buy her car back," I refused, thus ending what had been a good arrangement for us both.

In hindsight, I was perhaps "hard-hearted," but I was bitterly disappointed by what she had done and felt betrayed just as my father had been years before. I'm reminded of something he said after the incident, "Son, it's never wrong to help others, but you can't save the world."

Perhaps that's true, but Jonas Salk prevented millions of people from getting polio with the vaccine he developed in 1953, and Edward Jenner's discovery led to the elimination of smallpox. So, shouldn't we do what we can to make a difference?

I believe that every act of kindness toward another, no matter how small, can make the world a better place in which to live. Something as simple as sharing a smile is an act of kindness, but its impact may be profound! Your smile might be the spark needed to lift a stranger out of a deep funk or give them a sense of self-worth or renewed hope. Some efforts are, perhaps, doomed to failure, but how do you know that in advance? It's better, I think, to take a risk, and do something positive for your fellow man. Who knows? What you do may not save the world, but it might make a difference in the life of the person you helped.

ABOUT THE AUTHOR

Since 1994, Wayne has been sharing his wit and wisdom with students, educators, and dental professionals across the U. S. and Canada. Although he generally speaks on scientific topics or practice management, his presentations on "Life Skills" seem to resonate with audiences everywhere. His books, *"When Mom and Dad Need Help,"* and *"When Life Needs a Sticky Note"* were written in response to almost universal interest.

"Wise Words from Lessons Learned," was inspired by the many snippets of wisdom offered to Wayne as a youth by his father, J. C. Kerr, Jr. Many of these words of advice contributed to his core values and character, and it is his belief that, by sharing, others can benefit as well. *"It's Okay to be Square"* expands on that theme, and introduces additional concepts embraced by the author.

As a professional, Wayne earned numerous honors, including Fellowship in both the American and International Colleges of Dentistry, the Pierre Fauchard Academy, as an Honored Fellow of the Georgia Dental Association, Mastership in the Academy of General Dentistry, and as a recipient of the Academy's Life-Long Learning and Service Recognition Award.

As a community volunteer, Wayne has been recognized as Professional, Citizen, Volunteer, and Small-business Person of the Year. Additionally, he was honored by the Georgia Institute of Technology with its presentation of the Dean Griffin Community Service Award. Working with other community leaders, Wayne helped found a clinic for the indigent providing free dental and medical services.

Retired from clinical care, Wayne's passion is to shorten the learning curve to success for other dentists and their team members. He is an Adjunct Associate Professor for the University of Alabama's School of Dentistry, helps prepare dental hygiene students for their National Board Exam (www.dhseminars.com), speaks on a variety of topics for major dental meetings, and posts a monthly blog called kerrthoughts. Archived blogs are available at www.kerrspeak.com as well as other resources for practice building, or text the word kerrspeak to 22828 to access a link to sign up for his commentary on the first Thursday of every month. Contact Wayne by email at wayne@kerrspeak.com.

61306463R10046